God Is Always Good

My Life, Business and How You can do it Too!

David B. Taylor

I dedicate this book to my Mother, La Juana Prior, and Grandmother, Joy Williams. If it wasn't for these two women none of this would be possible.

I Love You Both

Contents

Introduction 9

Failure Is Not an Option ………………….. 17

Cali Life ……………………............……25

Good Ole Montana ………………......….33

Going Back to Cali …………………….39

The Worst News of My Life ………………51

Another Trial ……………………………71

Back Sliding ……………………………79

Clothing Store……………………………89

T - Shirt Business Check List ……………101

Marketing Your Business ……………......107

Instagram ……………………….........…115

3 Things to be successful

In business………………………….......121

The purpose of this book is not only to give you tools to start and market your own t-shirt business. It will also display my life's examples of some of the trials you will face, which will prepare you for business. My intention is to display how only faith, consistency and continuing to grow as an individual will help you succeed."

Introduction

"When you decide not to grow only two things happen, you stay the same or you die"

I was born November 28th 1985 to La Juana Prior and David Taylor. My mother was a young, vibrant, beautiful woman. My father was a well-dressed, smooth talking business owner. As long as I can remember my mother was always a hard working woman, she worked anywhere and would do anything to provide for my two brothers and I. My father, well I can't remember much about him only memories of playing in my grandmother's living room and him giving my cousins and I money while we were playing on the corner at my Aunt's house. One day, he was found dead in my grandmother's house upstairs in a hot room due to drug overdose. As I write, tears begin to pour down my eyes because I wonder how different my life would have been if he had been a part of it. I heard many stories of him, how he was a great man. How he owned a liquor store, hotel and a game room. He also did community work with AIDS patients. He was an avid reader and a scholar, graduating from Houston Tillotson University and was a member of Alpha Phi Alpha fraternity. He also sold albums, eight tracks and cassette tapes out of his liquor store. He loved music, and was a light in the life of whoever he came in contact with; I again wonder how different my life would have been. My mother, when I think of her I just smile. She was such a great, honest, loving but stern person. She showed me how much she loved me with her actions, not so much by her words. She was the definition of hustle and hard work; her life really showed me how to love not only your children but your family also. She was the type of woman who wasn't afraid to tell you when you're wrong. I cannot remember one time she did not hold herself accountable for her own actions. Growing up my mother was always working and I was mostly taken care of by my grandmother, Joy Williams. I would call her "Mama Joy," because she was not only like a mother to me but she was my joy. She was also a very hard working woman; she owned her own barber shop and was one of the first black female barbers in Galveston, TX. She was the foundation of who I would become as a person and a man. When I was young she would have me answering the telephone at her barber shop "Joy's Hair World". I would also sweep the shop and do whatever other duties she needed me to do. Here at this shop was where one of my first entrepreneurial experiences happened. A couple of years ago I was attending church at St. Luke Baptist Church in Galveston and one of the members a former client of my grandmother told me a story. One day while she was getting her hair styled I came into the barber shop with a huge smile on my face and a hand full of money. I had to be no older than 7 years old. My grandmother asked how I got all that money, come to find out I was parking cars behind her barber shop and charging people. It was Mardi Gras weekend in Galveston and I guess I believed people needed somewhere to park, and I needed money. Joy would always tell me growing up one day I would have a big office with a nice name plate on the front of my desk. I would make her vision come to pass several times over.

It is really important what you speak into the lives of your children at a young age because they will somehow never forget it.

Mama Joy was also the foundation of my faith. I began my walk with Christ at Market Street Baptist Church in Galveston, TX. The Pastor was Reverend Thomas at that time. It was a wood framed church that sat on the corner. The inside of the church was also all wood. I remember Reverend Thomas; he had a caramel brown complexion and white hair, a whole head of it. He wore suspenders and I remember telling my grandmother I wanted to dress just like Reverend Thomas for church on Sundays, so she dressed me just like him. At Market Street Church I would be baptized and filled with the Holy Spirit, since then I have walked with Christ. I thank God for Joy.

David B. Taylor

Failure Is Not an Option

"If it's not happening, make it happen"

As a teenager I was a different type of guy, I always had a strong desire to work for everything. I never counted on anyone to get things done for me. Something inside of me knew if I wanted anything in life I would have to get it myself. <u>Nothing worth having is handed to you.</u> The year before high school, at about 14 years old, Mama Joy passed from a two year fight with lung cancer; this would be my first encounter with the disease. When she passed she left me about $500.00 dollars. I used the money to get my driver's permit and bought my first car (yes at the age of 14). Man did my mother beat me! The car, a 1985 Oldsmobile Toronado, was only $275.00. I still own one to this day, it reminds me of that time in my life. I guess I always had my priorities in order even though we didn't have much growing up.

I remember in my middle school years there was a time we had small mice running around our house like it was a race track. There was an instance I came home from school and the lights were cut off, so I just laid down and went to sleep. These challenges gave me the passion to never want to experience these things in my adult life. So I always found a way to get what I needed done. Parking those cars had taught me something.

High school was fun. I was an all-around athlete, played all sports and embodied the typical football jock mentality. I messed with as many girls as possible and had a very arrogant attitude. I choose football as the sport I would pursue. My senior year, I was an All-Conference selection on both sides of the field, but with a 2.1 GPA and no football scholarship due to me not having the grades to qualify for any. This was the first major blow, the first trial that would show me who I was as a person and where my heart and faith in myself rested.

I wasn't giving up, so I made a highlight tape and my friend Delvin and I went to every school up Interstate 45 and dropped one off. We went so far we made it to Dallas, where I met with Coach Archie

Cooley of Paul Quinn College. He saw my tape and loved it, and said if he could he would have given me a scholarship right then. Due to grade issues I would have to sit out my first season, but if I got good grades I would be able to play in the spring.

I live by the motto *"If it's not happening make it happen"*. I had been given a chance, so I applied and was accepted into the school and spent my first college semester there. But the school was not up to the standards I set for myself, and I struggled with that. Somedays in the dorms we would have to take cold showers, due to not having hot water. Because of my higher dreams, I decided to not go out for the football team as planned... I just saw more for my life and football career. After that first semester I returned home to Galveston, and attended the local community college until I figured out what I wanted to do. Then one day while at a little league baseball game, a former high school coach told me he knew of a school in California called Butte College. He spoke with the coaching staff, and couple of months later I was on a plane leaving my family behind and going to an unknown place. Unknown was always good for me. It was a fresh start and a new opportunity.

Cali Life

"I thank God for always taking me through trials, because what they did was strengthen my faith and made me continue to put my trust in Him"

I remember the first day I arrived in California. I was picked up by the defensive coordinator, Coach Modes, and dropped off in an apartment with about 20 other guys. I instantly knew something had to change. A guy I knew from my home town, Jamal, was also attending the same college, and we soon found out we were cousins. He had some family members who lived there, Garrick and Cat, so naturally I went with them. Garrick and Cat...I thank God for these two men taking me in, no telling where I would be today without them... but God always made a way.

One of the first conversations Jamal and I had with Cat, he said, "One of you will make it out of here, and one of you will not". I decided that day I would be the one to make it out. I quickly started figuring out what he meant though. Another nearby university, Chico State, was one of the top party schools in the nation. Drugs and parties were the norm so it was very easy to get trapped. I would end up getting trapped in both.

My football career was going well, I made the team after about 130 people tried out and more than half were cut. I started the season second on the depth chart behind a senior. After about the fourth game of the season, I went to a party on the weekend and was jumped by nine people. I remember waking up in the middle of the street, drunk with blood rushing out of a hole in the side of my mouth, and a huge cut over my knee. I had drove a friend's car there, and I jumped in it and drove to her house bloody and all. When I arrived she made me go to the hospital and I was rushed into surgery. My football season was over and maybe even my football career. My mother flew to California to be with me while I recovered, and I returned home to Texas for a little while. A couple of months later I found out one of the guys busted a bottle over my knee (while I was unconscious), intentionally trying to end my football career.

In life and business there will be people who want to secretly end your career. These people come in the form of friends, family members and other businesses. It is solely up to you how you react to these situations, will you be defeated or walk into your greatness?

Now was the time to make a decision: give up or press forward. While at home in Texas, I continued to study for my classes and completed my school work. I returned to California on crutches. I was not willing to give up everything I worked so hard for. God had a plan for me to play football. I started physical therapy, and continued for a couple months until I slowly began to walk again, healing to the point that I no longer needed crutches. Around this time, I started attending a little church in Chico. I knew only God could get me through this. That spring, I was back on the football field! This was the second time I overcame the odds. My faith was once again tested and I graduated to another level.

David B. Taylor

My final year of football at Butte College was good, even though we did not have great season as a team. I was voted First Team All-Conference, and accepted an athletic scholarship to Montana State University in Bozeman, MT. I was headed to another unfamiliar place by myself, blindly following God's path for me.

David B. Taylor

Good Ole Montana

"You have to make a choice whether to dwell on your mistakes, or live for your future"

Playing at Montana State I accomplished so much on the football field that going into my senior year I was one of the top corners in the Big Sky Conference. But after the first couple of games in the season, Hurricane Ike hit Galveston and destroyed most of the island and thousands of homes. My mother and family were still living there. I had a heavy sense of anxiety because I wanted to make sure they were ok. At this same point in the year, I was also suffering from a bad pain in my hand due to something happening on the football field. So going into a game against Eastern Washington, a game we needed to win to have any chance at the playoffs, I was carrying a load of stress. This game would prove to be the 3rd major setback of my life at this point. In the fourth quarter, with about 2 minutes left in the game, while the offense was on the field and we were down by three touchdowns, there were guys on the team laughing on the sideline. I remember how bad I wanted to win that game and how much I sacrificed playing with this hand injury and everything that was going on in my life. I began to yell at them. Then I found myself yelling at the coaches, which lead to me walking to the locker room across the street from the stadium. My position coach watched me leave the stadium from the press box. I packed my things and went home, sealing the fate of my football career. I was dismissed from the team, publicly humiliated, and lived with a broken spirit for a long time. All my hopes and dreams of a career in the NFL were thrown down the drain because I let my emotions get the best of me. To this day I don't live life with regrets; I believe it was a lesson I needed to learn. *Do not let your emotions get the best of you.* You will most likely make the wrong decision - this relates to business and life. I had to come to terms with what I'd done. I had to continue to go to school and face the other football players who looked at me in disgust. I knew I had to attain my college degree. I could not have spent all this time to leave with nothing! So I continued to work hard in the classroom, and that spring graduated with my degree.

Do not let tragic circumstances crush your dreams. The most successful people in life are great at dusting themselves off and moving to the next thing.

Going Back To Cali

"You will never achieve anything great in life without struggle, perseverance and a whole gallon of faith"

During those years in college, I was working with a guy from back home in Texas, Matt. He was a friend of my brother, and wanted to start a mobile auto detailing business. After I graduated from Montana State, I moved home to Galveston and started working with him in a 50/50 partnership. We did very well, I remember in the first 6 months we made about

$40,000. We worked together for about a year until I decided I wanted to move back to California. I just knew there was more out there for me. This business had given me the confidence to go into any field of business and believe I could succeed.

Be sure you're always on the same page in a partnership and your desires and aspirations for the business are the same, or it will not work.

I packed my car with everything I owned and $1,800 and set out to California. The plan was to live with a friend of the family when I got there, until I could afford my own place. Thirty five hours of driving later, I arrived in San Jose, CA. I remember pulling up to the front of my friend's house and couldn't wait to unload my car, but he wasn't home at this time. So I called him, and he told me where the key was and I went in to the house. When I got in, I was confronted by an angry woman. I told her the situation and how he told me I could live there...but she didn't know, and it was her house! I was kicked out my first day there without a place to live. I remember during this time my mother calling and asking if everything was ok and I would lie and say I was doing great. I didn't want her to worry. I found a friend of mine I knew was living in the area at the same time. It was actually the same girl who had let me borrow her car that night I was jumped in Chico. She allowed me to live with her for a couple of weeks until I found a job and a place to live.

One day during a conversation, she told me I should have never moved to Silicon

Valley. That maybe I should go home, because I was in over my head. That night I remember praying to God in tears asking him to help me make it. I knew God had something for me in Silicon Valley. The next week, I had a couple of interviews. I believed because I had a college degree and previously owned my own business I felt entitled to a high paying job. I felt I shouldn't wear anything less than a suit and tie to work, but boy was I wrong.

It is not really about how many degrees you have... but are you hard working and willing to learn? This is what will get you far in life.

I went to the first interview, and had another one scheduled to work for a corporate housing company as a cleaner. I made my mind up before the first interview I would not go to the second. But I changed my mind, and I decided to go to the second interview. I remember being in the room and looking at the management and the people who were around me and thinking, "I could move up fast, if I put in the time". It was a worldwide company with a lot of opportunity. I was hired the same day; I returned to my friend's house and looked on Craigslist for roommates in the area my new job was. It wasn't long before I found new roommates and a place to live. A week later I moved out and was living with my new roommates. I did all this with only $1800. For the first month, I slept on the floor until I was able to buy an air mattress. I didn't have a lot, but it was mine. After my first check I was able to buy a mattress from someone selling them out of an alley, a TV, Dresser, and TV Stand. Working at the cleaning company was hard work and long hours, for $13.00 per hour. Some days I would work 16 hours, and 140 hours for two weeks. I knew there had to be a better way of doing things. There was no reason for us to work like slaves. I made a vow that day that I would get promoted and make a change.

About 6 months later, while in the warehouse, I got the opportunity to speak to the divisional manager. I told him my background and how I could make a change in the company, and the inefficient things saw and how to make them better. A month later, I was promoted to assistant manager over the second largest property in the company! The property was big but also one of the worst in the company for the past 20 years. However, I saw its potential, and after being there for only 6 months we won Property of the Year. I was then promoted to managing the entire cleaning department for that property. We continued to win award after award, and I was voted MVP of the Year for company.

After 6 months of managing that property, the company who owned the property decided they would no longer allow our company to oversee so many units. There was the same issue with another complex in the area. At this time, more than 600 units had to be unfurnished and given back to the property. I took over this project, and was promoted again to managing both properties in that area. While I was managing both properties, our company opened a new warehouse in the area to service all of Silicon Valley, and guess who they choose to run it AND the properties: ME!

You will never achieve anything great in life without struggle, perseverance and a whole gallon of faith.

Imagine if I would have listened to what my friend told me...that I was in over my head and needed to go home. I would have missed out on all that personal growth and management experience. But I knew God was big enough to get me through. I had prayed, and relied on my faith. *You will have a lot of people who will say you're not good enough or you can't do it. These people believe it can't be done because they don't see themselves accomplishing it.*

David B. Taylor

The Worst News of My Life

"Sometimes God has a blessing for us but we are just out of place to receive it"

One morning while at work I received a phone call from my older brother. My mother had experienced a seizure in the shower and was rushed to the hospital. A couple of hours later, we found out she had cancerous tumors on her brain. I remember instantly breaking down crying in my office. I called my girlfriend, Holly, and told her what happened and to book me a plane ticket to leave the same day. I arrived in Texas the same day to be with my mother before she went into brain surgery. The next day she was out and recovering well, but she still had a long way to go with radiation. Unfortunately, after further tests we were informed the doctors discovered she had stage four lung cancer and it had spread from her lungs to her brain. The doctors gave her four months to live.

Once my mother was able to return home, I returned to California. I would talk to my mother every day. She would tell me how she didn't want me to give up the life I worked so hard for. Yet I knew on the inside she needed me there. We always had such a special relationship. I knew she would always support me no matter what, but she also wasn't afraid to tell me if I was being selfish or unreasonable. I really leaned on her in everything I did. We would talk on the phone sometimes for hours, just laughing. Other times while on the phone, I would read her scriptures from the Bible to encourage her. We would talk about how we would go to church together when I returned to Texas.

I had told Holly upon returning to California that I needed to move to Texas to be with my mother. She understood and completely agreed. Amazingly, the lease for our apartment was up the same month, and I also received a credit card that helped pay for the moving company. During my previous trip to Texas, I had started planning ahead and looking for duplexes. I had found one but someone had already submitted their application before me. But then I received a phone call: the person did not qualify and the place was ours! It was amazing how God lined up everything for me to move. *A lot of the time God has a blessing for us but we are not in the right place to receive it.*

A couple of weeks passed by and Holly and I drove from California to Texas in two separate cars. I thank God for Holly and her support, because she did not have to move with me. Holly had already left her family in Seattle once to be with me in the Bay Area. I remember telling her she didn't have to move and I understood if she wanted to go back to her own family. But we were in love, and she decided she would stick by me the entire time; a decision that made me love her even more. I will always cherish her for that choice.

God will always honor a person when they do things out of sincerity and to serve others. We are not to give or do anything which seems from the heart, but is not of the heart.

I was back in Texas, the place I vowed to never move back to after I had left the second time. But this time was different, I was there to be by my mother's side and help her fight her bout with cancer. Upon arriving in Galveston, Holly and I decided we needed to go and look for jobs. That very first day we both went out and received jobs at hotels. I received a position working at Hotel Galvez as the Housekeeping Manager. It was amazing, they had actually denied my application when I applied online, so I went and spoke directly with the hiring person in Human Resources. After speaking with her, I received an interview with Ms. Washington, who was actually only there until the new Director of Housekeeping arrived. I interviewed with her, the Director of Rooms and the General Manager of the hotel. Within one week I was working at the hotel. The hotel had hired a new Director before I was hired, but she wouldn't start until around the same time I did. The lady did not take a liking to me from the first moment we met. She actually tried to fire me and have me escorted out of the building during a disagreement we had. The next day, I received a call from the GM and was able to return to work. But for the next two months I was to spend my time working in the laundry.

I always found myself going back to serve, to be among the outcast and people who others had wrote off. Because of this I was taught a great lesson in leadership and people in general. You cannot lead until you're willing to follow and serve, leadership is servitude.

In a matter of a month, I turned the laundry around to the point we could close it and things still got done. No matter where I was, I always wanted to do the best job as possible. While dealing with everything at work, I would speak to my mother and she would always say, "David you need to quit that job". But I knew one day there would be a funeral I would have to pay for, so I needed to endure this. I remember taking her to radiation treatments every day, and encouraging her get out the house and do things to get her mind off what was taking place. There had been some complications after her brain surgery. She should have received radiation within a couple of days following the procedure, but due to lack of insurance they denied her. So I wrote a four page letter to UTMB, discussing how she was treated and didn't receive proper care after her surgery. Because of my efforts, she was granted full health coverage. One particular day, we were walking out of the doctor's office after her treatment and my mother was in tears. I asked her what was wrong, and she replied, "David those people were just going to let me die, I'm happy you came here". Just to be there for her like she had always been for me, it meant the world to me. There was nothing else I could do to relate to that feeling.

When we got home that day, I asked her if she remembered our plans to go to church together. The first Sunday that I was back home, she didn't get up for church. The second Sunday was Mother's Day, and she was able to come with me to church. While sitting in the service, I could see it on her face: she was really enjoying it. It was making a change in her on the inside. That day, she gave her life to Christ and two weeks later she was baptized! It's funny how God works, because the Pastor was actually on vacation, and he came back just to baptize my mother. What if I decided not to move back to Texas, unaware I was the person God would use to help my mother find her salvation? I was the person to bring her to church so she could be saved. I believe to this day if I would have stayed in California, my life would have been cursed.

A short time after this, she started to receive radiation on her lung. Due to the treatment a tube was placed in her lung, and it had to be drained every day or she would drown on her own fluid. It was so hard seeing her going through that. Sitting on the bed in the hospital, she hugged me while telling me how she was in so much pain. That she wanted to die; she wanted the doctors to kill her. I think at this time she was ready to go, to get it over with, she had made her peace with God. Eventually she was sent home on hospice care and my brothers and family took turns taking care of her. I remember in her last days she was walking back and forth in the same spot sitting, standing, crossing her legs for 24 hours straight. It stopped when her body could no longer move and she tried to get up but couldn't. The night before she died we had family members over. We sat outside and talked about all the good times we had with her, laughed, and listened to music. The next morning I remember waking up and she was still alive. I was to the point I was tired of seeing her suffer and I wanted her pain to be gone. Before going to work I whispered to her in her ear, "I love you, and don't worry I will take care of my brothers. It's ok to let go". I drove 10 mins away to work at the hotel, and 10 mins later I received the call that she died. My older brother and I paid for majority of the funeral expenses, and her funeral was packed to the point that more chairs had to be brought in. People spoke very highly of my mother at the funeral, saying so many wonderful things about the person she was. I remember thinking I want people to think of me like this when I die.

The day after my mother was buried, I returned to work. People could not understand how I did it; I guess I felt like working would help me deal with it better than sitting at home. I had no regrets about my mother, I knew how she felt about me and she knew how I felt about her. She instilled things in me which could never be taken away. I can still hear her voice in my head saying "hey honey" whenever she answered the phone. I continued to work at the hotel for some time after that. The Director who tried to fire me fell down the stairs and had a seizure. She was eventually fired for not being able to complete the tasks of the job. I was then promoted to Director; remember the Bible says God will make your enemies your footstool. I honestly think my mother had something to do with that, it sounds like something she would do (I'm smiling right now).

Under my leadership we were able to take the department ranking from the mid-70s in the nation to number 11. I had a great mentor at the time in Ms. Barbra Washington. She was hard on me, always telling me to shut up when I thought I knew something. I needed those hard lessons, she taught me how to be quiet and learn. She would say, "The more you learn David, the more you will be able to place in your tool belt to use when you leave here". She reminded me so much of my grandmother Joy, she was exactly who I

needed at the time. God always found a way to surround me with the right people at the right times.

A couple of months later I decided to leave my job at the hotel. I have an inner complex - when I accomplish something difficult, I have to move on to the next thing. I have never been the type of person to settle for anything. *I believe your spirit starts to die when you stop trying to improve yourself.*

David B. Taylor

Another Trial

"Trials are just God's way of strengthen our faith" But God...

Once again I was on the job hunt. I had money saved at this time so it was not as stressful. But I was ready to get back to work. I never really took time to reflect on my mother passing away or anything that happened in the past year. I would just work my way through it. After being on the hunt for a job for a couple of weeks, I received a job working at Aaron's Sales and Lease. I was back again starting at the bottom, a manager in training, after leaving a job that paid me about $70,000 a year. But I was tired of working in leadership positions at the time; I didn't want to manage people. Instead I wanted to go to work, do a job and go home. I was back dealing with another bad supervisor, I took a pay cut and was only making $15.00 per hour, but I was happy. At this job God was giving me time to heal and get past some things. I finally had the time to concentrate on my own dreams. I got in the habit of taking setbacks in life head on because every time it seemed like God demoted me financially, he promoted me later on.

I would constantly think of different businesses I could start, I had my mind set on a club or a liquor store, something I knew would make money fast. One day before I went to bed I prayed for God to give me a business. I woke up at 3:00am that morning with the "God Is Good" logo in my head. I went upstairs and tried to draw what I had envisioned, and when I finally set down my pencil, it was perfect!

See God will give you a vision but he always gives you the means to get it done. Also, if your vision is not working, check to make sure it is yours and of God. You see, a couple years prior in California I was working to start my own magazine. While doing this I bought all the proper equipment to design, so I had everything I needed. God had it already lined up for me! *When you're walking in your purpose, it doesn't take much to get great things done.*

The next day I sent the drawing to Vista Print to be placed on a t-shirt, hat, pen, notepad, and handbag. It was about an $80.00 investment. When I received the items back I knew I was on to something, so I searched for a local screen printer and printed about 50 shirts. That weekend I advertised the shirts on Facebook and sold all 50 of them. I was going to houses dropping them off, meeting people places, going to barbershops, banks, and hair salons, anywhere I thought someone would buy a shirt. I did this while working at Aaron's for a couple of months, but it was a lot of work doing both. I went from buying 50 to 100 to 250 shirts at a time.

At that point, I decided to leave Aaron's and get another job, the money just wasn't worth the time. I had just bought a new house, so my expenses were pretty high. I filled out an application for a recycling company for the Market Manager positon, and was called the same day. I interviewed the next day and was hired immediately. My salary almost doubled compared to the hotel!

David B. Taylor

I have learned over the past years that before God promotes you, he always demotes you first. I guess it is to see if you will love him the same when you have less.

Back Sliding

"It is better to go through failures, then to look back and never have tried"

After getting the new job, I don't know if it was the money or what, but everything that was going on the past couple of years began to catch up with me. I fell into a deep depression and started drinking and going out a lot. The hurt and the pain of my mother passing away, and also the disappointments of other people in my life started to weigh on me. I stopped putting much effort into my new clothing company, which I had recently named Godly Creations Clothing. I lost all my motivation around this time. Maybe because I wasn't living right I felt like I shouldn't be selling Godly apparel. I guess I hadn't fully learned from the other failures in my life.

Just because things aren't going well, never stop working on yourself and your dreams.

It was New Years of 2014 and I decided I would do something different. I started going to a new church, Word of

Restoration, by invite of my friend Delvin. Delvin was same guy who rode with me when I was handing out video tapes to colleges while trying to get a scholarship. The church really changed my life. At this time Holly became pregnant, and we both rededicated our lives back to Christ. I joined the choir a short time after this. One day while sitting outside the church waiting on choir practice to start, my friend Austin Rice brought up the clothing company and asked me "why did you stop it? It was such a good thing". I remember thinking to myself - why did I stop? From that day forward I began to put all my focus back into Godly Creations Clothing. In February of 2015, I set a goal and wrote down that by August I wanted to have my own store. The Bible says to write the vision. It is very important you write down your goals and aspirations for life. Envision yourself in the positions you desire so they can manifest. You have to see yourself there to get there. By August 1, 2015 Godly Creations Clothing in Hitchcock, TX opened its doors. Whenever

God is trying to do something in your life he always sends a man, and the man he sent at that time was Austin.

A couple of months prior to opening the store, I received a large increase on one of my credit cards. I remember sitting on the couch and telling Holly, "I don't even need all this money"... but God had a plan for it. I also was supposed to get a large bonus from work which had been held up for some time. I remember driving down Highway 6 and seeing this shopping center, but I just didn't believe it was the place for my store. But around June, I decided if I was going to meet my August deadline I had to start moving. I told myself if the guy who owns the shopping center would give me some time to set up my business first without paying for the month, then it was meant to be. To my surprise and through God's vision, the man said yes. I gave him the down payment (which was about $2,000), and I began to buy everything needed for the store. It's amazing how God gave me the unexpected increase in funds the previous month. At the time I didn't know what to do with it, and then my bonus came that month too. God was supplying everything I needed to open my business!

On July 17, 2015 my son David Jr was born, and I remember the day after he was born leaving the hospital and running to the store and setting things up. I knew how dedicated I had to be. August 1st arrived quickly, and I remember praying in the back of the store early that morning for people to show up. It was a great Grand Opening with about $1,000 in sales that day, from only about 15 to 20 customers. I knew then God was really with me! When I returned to my other job, I knew I could no longer be there. My spirit was telling me it was time to go, and that day I placed my resignation. Shortly after I removed all the money out of my 401K and prepared my family and I for the long, hard journey of entrepreneurship.

Life is too short to live afraid, it is better to go through failures, then to look back and never have tried. The only thing to fear is fear its self.

Business Life

Godly Creations Clothing Store

"Anything gained overnight is not worth having"

It was extremely hard owning my own business again in the beginning; especially the first three months. One of the main factors was not just sales, but getting out of the paycheck-to-paycheck mentality. I was so use to my bills being paid ahead of time and always having extra money.

When you start your own business all your money goes to it. I really don't believe in part time businesses: you're either all in or all out. When you first start out you believe it will happen one way, but as soon as you get into it you see it another way. Don't have your heart set on making any real profit from your business until after the first year.

As the brand continued to grow the amount of money I spent on inventory did the same. The pattern was the same with customers...more customers equaled more demand, which equaled more money spent on inventory. My overhead expenditures also grew. When your product line expands, it means you will need to buy more hangers, clothing racks, price tags etc. So basically the first six months you are building the store, and also driving the brand to the maximum capacity of the store. I invested so much more of my money into the business then it made. I learned the more merchandise you have to sell, the more your cost per order will increase. But it hurts when you don't have the customer base to buy the product or the product goes cold (doesn't sell). The first 4 months of the business we only made about $12,000 over that period, which barely paid the expenses (and don't think about paying yourself). During that initial period of your business, you have to adapt and learn fast. As previously stated, our problem was not having enough inventory selection. Our customers were limited to only the 8 or 9 designs we had in the store at that time. When we started expanding our designs and products, I learned that whenever you are growing your product selection that also increases your inventory expenses, and it has to grow inversely with your customer base. I learned when I first started I had to put out new colors and different styles to attract new customers and figure out what people like. I tell people all the time, business people learn with a whole lot of money involved. But in failure is the prize, because you know not to make that mistake again. By November I figured it out. I now understood what sold and what didn't, and was able to have inventory in the merchandise that did sell and discontinued the merchandise that didn't.

When I started my website, I learned this is a little different online: only sell your top selling products and introduce new products that will appeal to the masses. You will usually always have more new customers online then returning customers. Another big thing is do not be afraid to have an advertised sale, every large department store does it. It is the way you move non-selling merchandise or the last of stock to make room for new stock.

Do not get in the habit of thinking your product is too good or the demand is too high to not have a sale. After I learned this principle I was able to go into December and January making over $10,000 in just those two months. These numbers might sound small to some, but you have to remember we are selling our own products. It is totally different from a store selling well known products of someone else. From that point on we never saw another month under $3,000 again!

God always sent people to me with a word of encouragement. Some people would give me $100 just to bless me. As Les Brown says, "I was behind on my bills and my dreams" at this time. I was offered to go back to my old job, which I turned down. There were many times I wanted to give up and quit. It would have been easier on me and my family just to get a regular job. I will never forget this one time that December, I spent all the money I had on inventory (I literally had only one dollar left in my pocket), about $2,000. But for some reason I had such an ease and calmness over me. I remember telling my aunt about this over the phone, and saying "God will provide". You see, I would have hated not to be able to afford to get my son anything for his for first Christmas because I took a chance with his Christmas money. But the next two days, the store made about $3,000!

Always trust your gut, it is God trying to relay a message or to guide you in the right direction. That wasn't the last time I would only have a dollar left and surely not the last time I would be late on my bills.

While back at the store, I was working on growing my social media base and online sales, which are not easy when you have a limited budget. The major thing to be successful in these times is to have a large social media base. You not only receive orders but it builds your credibility as a brand. I would definitely tell a person who wants to open their own store to make sure their online sales alone can cover their business expenses (rent, utilities, etc.).

David B. Taylor

When I first started the store, I didn't know much about retail other than the store I worked at in college. Then to have such a unique product, that was a double mistake. Thus I had to learn quickly as I went, which to me is the best way to learn. Everyone's businesses are different but the principals are the same. I learned what worked best and most cost effectively, and we have actually closed our retail store now after one full year and over $50,000 in sales. We have moved to more of an online based company and also have a store inside of a hospital in the Houston area. "Go where the traffic is, it is easier than creating traffic." Since we have made this change sales have went through the roof.

By using the wisdom and guidelines I placed in these stories, you are sure to have your own successful retail store or online business in no time. I have laid out the most important steps in the following pages.

How to Start Your Own T - Shirt

Business: The Check List

1. Get a GREAT design! If you can't design, then find someone who can create your vision in your style. (Cost is free to no more than $250 max) Don't worry so much about trademarks and etc. If your shirt takes off then use the profit from your shirts to get it done. Just get started!
2. Find a local Screen Printer. Search online for someone local or you can use Vista Print. I refer people to

theprintboxx.com they can get any of your needs taken care of.

3. Have a mock shirt made (Black shirts sell the most) It should cost about $30 max to make one shirt. Be sure to have it produced exactly the way you want it when you start to sell.

4. Show the mock shirt to friends and family and persons on social media who can care less what you think. A lot of people will support you because it's you. The most important thing you need to know is do you have a product

that can be sold to people who do not know you.

5. Go to beauty salons, barber shops and different places you believe those people would wear your product. Try to sell to them and figure how much they are willing to pay for it. Ask them to give you any feedback about your product.

6. Concentrate on selling one design when you start off; it is better to have one good design, then to have 4 bad

and 1 good. You will waste a lot of money trying to sell bad product.

7. File for a DBA at your local courthouse so you can receive your product at wholesale price (costs about $25 to file for a DBA or Assumed Name)

8. Build a website using a platform which is easy to learn on your own, to customize and update yourself. Bigcartel.com and Shopify.com are great platforms to start your website. You will spend a lot of money starting

off hiring a web designer, and might not get the results you want. There is always YouTube University, do not be afraid to use it to learn. (Shopify costs $15-$120 a month, Big Cartel costs about $10-$60 a month). You will also have to buy a domain name which costs about $15 per year; I recommend namecheap.com for this.

9. Set up Google Analytics and Mail Chimp account for your site. Analytics will tell you the locations of the persons coming to your website,

demographics and etc. Mail Chimp is for building an email list and making it possible to mass email everyone on your email list, both are free of cost.

10. Get a Stamps.com account for shipping, the cost is way cheaper than going to USPS but you will need a laser printer, shipping labels and shipping bags. You can get all this on Amazon.com. (Stamps account is about $16 per month. Labels, bags and a printer are about $75 total)

Marketing Your Business

I have tried several different approaches in advertising other than social media: Google Ad Words, Ad Words Express, and Yelp. But Facebook has by far produced the best results. First thing, set up a Facebook Business Page; this will allow you to pay for advertising. The great thing about Facebook advertising is the customer will see your product and you are able to know if a post is doing well fairly quickly. Whenever you advertise a post on Facebook, a good indicator is how many likes it gets. Your total amount of likes should be at least 10% of the reach of your post. Example, if your post has reached 50K people you should have at least 5K likes. In Facebook, you are able to set the demographics of your post. You need to know your target market and exactly who you want to reach. You can find this information using Google Analytics. I have found you get the best results by boosting a post without having a "buy me now button" or "offer now button". If you have a nice picture advertised, people will want to expand the picture but will go to your website, and this makes for a lot of useless traffic. The "Buy Now Posts" I believe come off too "selly" and people do not really react to them versus the regular Facebook boost which solely has a picture and caption. By doing it this way you will get tons of likes and shares if you have a nice product. You will only do as well as the product you are selling, do not give people low quality products and expect great results. ALWAYS PLACE YOUR WEBSITE ADDRESS IN THE CAPTION.

When making a caption for your post try to sell the item like you would in person. For example, if you were selling at a booth and a person wanted your product but couldn't purchase at that time. What would you say to get them to buy something from your website? For example you would say, "All our shipping is free, here is a coupon code" and offer a free gift with their first purchase? These are things that will motivate someone to actually go to your site and make a purchase if they truly like your product. Once you find a great picture and caption, stick with it; be sure it is making the 10% threshold before you place any real money into it. To test this, boost a post for $20 for one day, and see the reaction you receive. Another great thing about boosting posts in this fashion is you get "page likes". The more page likes you have the less money you will have to spend on boosting posts. You will then be able to post to your business page and get likes. Good ads over a long period of time work best. Meaning boosting for an entire month vs short ads for a day or two are better because the post gains momentum over time. To test, you should use short posts, and find out how well they perform and if you capture any converts you should use them over a long period of time. This is a game of consistency it will not happen overnight; you have to do it over a couple of month's period to see results. The more money you place into your ads the faster your page will grow; it all depends on how much you're willing to risk. Everything in life and business depends on you doing something about it. You must take action!

David B. Taylor

That is why faith without works is dead faith.

Instagram

Instagram is another great tool to capture sales, but it is only great depending on the number of followers you have. I would not recommend to place a lot of money into Instagram paid advertising because it burns up your money fast with little results. The same money will get you more results with Facebook. The way you gain followers on Instagram comes in several different ways. The first, liking the pictures of other users (but do not like random pictures). Only like pictures of people who would find interest in your product. For example, we sell God based clothing so we would look under hashtag "#God" and 'like' the pictures of those people. If they like what they see then they will follow you. The second way to gain followers is by following other people. Again you would go to a hashtag or a post of someone who would like the type of product you are selling and follow those people. If you follow or like the pictures of random people they will not follow you back because they probably are not interested in what you are selling. About 25% or less of the people you like pictures of, or follow will follow you back. Last, you can get shout outs from other accounts, sometimes it doesn't matter about how many followers a person has. It is just good to get your product in front of new faces. This is a game of consistently doing it every day. I recommend getting an Instagram Cleaner App so you can get rid of the people who are not following you back. You can mass unfollow instead of unfollowing people one by one. Good apps cost about a dollar and are well worth the money. There are ways you can cheat and get free followers but this is not effective because they are not real and fake people cannot buy your product or like your pictures. Hashtags are very important on Instagram, and you need to use hashtags every time you post. If you are not using hashtags you might as well not post.

Listed below are the top hashtags of 2016, make sure all of these are connected to your posts. Also add some of the key hashtags for the particular products you are selling. This allows your posts to show up everywhere and if people like your posts, they will like, and if they really like them they will follow you.

#love #me #tbt #cute #follow
#followme #photooftheday #happy
#tagforlikes #beautiful #girl #like
#selfie #picoftheday #summer #fun
#smile #friends #like4like #cat
#fashion #dog #baby #food

David B. Taylor

Top 3 Things to be Successful in Business

1 **Never be afraid of change, it doesn't matter what you like but what the customer likes. You might have a vision for your product, but if it is not getting a great response from your customer base then this means you have to change. Change is necessary in life to get you wherever you need to go. Don't have an issue with embracing it. If you refer back to my story you will see how God was always promoting me but it seemed as though**

he was demoting me. As my uncle Kevin would say "God only shines his light on your footsteps so you can see your next step, not your entire life at one time". Change was necessary in order for me to gain the tools I needed to succeed. You always have to produce what your customer wants. Be consistent in your service and everything you do. This trait, consistency, must become part of your life.

2. **Get connected with people in the same industry as you. They don't have to be more successful either. Other people can open your mind to new ideas and give a different version of the way you see things. Sometimes people have the best ideas, but don't have the "know how" to go about executing them. Recently I took on the mentorship of two clothing brands, and it really expanded my business. These two guys brought so much to the table with their passion and insight. We all**

needed to connect to take our businesses to the next level. There were things they tried and I learned from their mistakes and vice versa. The bible says "When two or more come together and agree of anything on Earth, it should be done by our Father in Heaven". Don't be afraid to connect with others just because you're in the same industry or business, it can save your business or take it to a new level. Whenever God wants to move you to another level he places a new person in your life to help you. If you shut every new person out of your life you might just miss who was sent to you from God.

3. Read! Read! Read! There is a mountain of information you can get from reading, you can be mentored by some of the greatest business people on earth by just turning a simple page. The average American reads one book a year. If you read one book in any subject a month, in five years you will be a master of that subject. "If you see a piece of paper on the

ground, pick it up and read it, for knowledge is everywhere".

Thank You

I truly thank everyone who has taken the time to read this book. I thank the people of Galveston County, friends, family and all the people around the world who have supported Godly Creations Clothing. I pray God blesses you and your families. I hope you were able to obtain some new knowledge from my writings, not only for your personal life but also your business life. The main point I wanted to convey in this book was for you to understand everything is possible with faith in God, action and hard work. When I reflect back on everything that has taken place in my life, I understand what God wanted to tell me...he was and is ALWAYS GOOD.

Don't forget to follow us ☺:

Facebook: Godly Creations Clothing

Instagram: @Godlycreationsclothing

Twitter: Godly_Creations

Email:Godlycreationsclothing@yahoo.com

www.ingramcontent.com/pod-product-compliance
Lightning Source LLC
Chambersburg PA
CBHW070257190526
45169CB00001B/449